AI Revolutionizes Pool Construction

Book Title:

The Future of Swimming Pools: AI-Driven Innovation in Construction

Chapters:

1. The Evolution of Swimming Pool Construction
2. Introduction to AI in Construction
3. AI Tools Revolutionizing Pool Design
4. Precision and Efficiency: AI in Pool Excavation
5. AI in Structural Engineering for Pools
6. Smart Materials: AI and Advanced Pool Materials
7. Enhancing Aesthetics with AI-Driven Design
8. AI in Water Management and Filtration Systems
9. Sustainable Pool Construction with AI
10. AI-Enhanced Safety Features for Pools
11. The Role of AI in Pool Maintenance
12. Case Studies: Successful AI-Driven Pool Projects
13. Challenges and Limitations of AI in Pool Construction
14. The Future Landscape of AI in Swimming Pools
15. Embracing AI: Training and Skills Development for Pool Professionals

Introduction:

In recent years, the construction industry has experienced a transformative shift with the integration of artificial intelligence

(AI). Among the various sectors benefiting from this technological revolution, swimming pool construction stands out as a field poised for significant advancements. The intersection of AI and swimming pool construction promises to enhance precision, efficiency, and creativity, leading to the development of state-of-the-art pools that meet the demands of modern consumers.

Swimming pools have evolved from simple backyard luxuries to sophisticated installations that require meticulous planning and execution. Traditionally, pool construction involved manual labor, extensive planning, and a considerable margin for error. However, with the advent of AI, the entire process has been reimagined. AI technologies are now being utilized to streamline every aspect of pool construction, from initial design to long-term maintenance.

One of the primary areas where AI has made a significant impact is in pool design. Advanced AI-driven software allows designers to create intricate and aesthetically pleasing pool layouts with unparalleled precision. These tools can simulate various design scenarios, providing clients with a virtual tour of their future pool and allowing for adjustments before the construction phase begins. This not only saves time and resources but also ensures that the final product aligns with the client's vision.

Beyond design, AI plays a crucial role in the excavation and structural engineering phases of pool construction. AI-powered machinery can perform excavation tasks with remarkable accuracy, reducing the risk of errors and minimizing environmental impact. Additionally, AI algorithms assist structural engineers in selecting the optimal materials and construction techniques, enhancing the overall durability and safety of the pool.

The materials used in pool construction have also seen a transformation thanks to AI. Smart materials, developed with the aid of AI, offer superior performance in terms of durability, maintenance, and environmental sustainability. These materials can adapt to changing conditions, such as water chemistry and temperature, ensuring the longevity and safety of the pool.

Water management and filtration systems have been revolutionized by AI as well. Traditional filtration systems often require frequent manual adjustments and maintenance. In contrast, AI-driven systems can monitor water quality in real-time and make necessary adjustments automatically. This not only ensures crystal-clear water but also reduces the need for chemical treatments, promoting a healthier swimming environment.

Sustainability is a growing concern in the construction industry, and AI is at the forefront of promoting eco-friendly practices in pool construction. From the use of recycled materials to the optimization of energy consumption, AI-driven solutions are making swimming pools more environmentally friendly. These advancements not only benefit the planet but also appeal to consumers who prioritize sustainability.

Safety is paramount in any pool construction project, and AI has introduced innovative safety features that were previously unimaginable. AI-powered sensors and monitoring systems can detect potential hazards, such as improper chemical levels or structural weaknesses, and alert pool owners in real-time. This proactive approach to safety minimizes risks and ensures a secure swimming environment for all users.

The role of AI extends beyond the construction phase to the maintenance of swimming pools. AI-driven maintenance systems can predict and address potential issues before they escalate, reducing downtime and maintenance costs. These systems can also provide pool owners with detailed insights into their pool's performance, allowing for informed decision-making regarding upgrades and repairs.

Throughout this book, we will delve into the various AI tools and technologies that are revolutionizing swimming pool construction. We will explore real-world case studies of successful AI driven pool projects, examine the challenges and limitations of implementing AI in this field, and discuss the future landscape of AI in swimming pool construction. By the end of this journey, you will have a comprehensive understanding of how AI is shaping the future of swimming pools and the opportunities it presents for both professionals and consumers.

Chapter 1: The Evolution of Swimming Pool Construction

Swimming pools have come a long way from their rudimentary beginnings to the sophisticated structures we see today. The history of swimming pool construction is a testament to human ingenuity and the relentless pursuit of luxury and recreation. This chapter takes you through the fascinating journey of swimming pool evolution, highlighting the significant milestones and technological advancements that have shaped the industry.

In ancient civilizations, swimming pools were a symbol of luxury and status. The Great Baths of Mohenjo-Daro, built around 2500 BCE in present-day Pakistan, are among the earliest examples of public water tanks used for bathing and social gatherings. Similarly, the ancient Greeks and Romans constructed elaborate pools for both athletic training and leisure. These early pools were primarily built using locally available materials such as stone and marble, and their construction relied heavily on manual labor.

The Renaissance period marked a resurgence of interest in swimming pools, particularly in Europe. The wealthy elite commissioned the construction of ornate pools in their estates, often adorned with intricate mosaics and sculptures. These pools were not only recreational spaces but also served as symbols of power and opulence. The construction techniques during this era remained labor-intensive, with skilled artisans playing a crucial role in creating these architectural marvels.

The advent of the 20th century brought significant changes to swimming pool construction. The development of new materials, such as reinforced concrete and gunite, revolutionized the industry. These materials offered greater flexibility in design and enhanced the durability of pools. The post-World War II era saw a surge in the popularity of residential swimming pools, driven by the booming economy and the rise of suburban living. Pool construction became more accessible to the general public, and standardization of designs and construction methods emerged.

The late 20th and early 21st centuries witnessed the integration of advanced technologies in swimming pool construction. Computer-aided design (CAD) software allowed for precise and efficient pool design, reducing the reliance on manual drafting. Hydraulic engineering advancements improved water circulation and filtration systems, enhancing the overall functionality of pools. Despite these technological strides, the construction process still involved a significant amount of manual labor and coordination among various trades.

Enter the era of artificial intelligence. The integration of AI in swimming pool construction is a game-changer, promising to redefine every aspect of the industry. From the initial design phase to the final touches, AI technologies are streamlining processes, enhancing precision, and reducing costs. AI-driven design software enables architects and designers to create intricate and personalized pool designs with ease. Machine learning algorithms analyze vast amounts of data to optimize construction techniques, ensuring the highest standards of quality and safety.

One of the most significant contributions of AI to pool construction is in the realm of excavation and structural engineering. AI-powered machinery can perform excavation tasks with unparalleled accuracy, minimizing the risk of errors and reducing environmental impact. Structural engineers leverage AI algorithms to select the best materials and construction methods, enhancing the durability and safety of pools. These advancements not only improve the efficiency of construction but also contribute to the sustainability of the industry.

As we move further into the 21st century, the potential for AI in swimming pool construction continues to expand. Innovations in smart materials, water management systems, and maintenance solutions are on the horizon, promising to elevate the standards of pool construction even higher. The future of swimming pools lies in the seamless integration of AI technologies, where creativity, efficiency, and sustainability converge to create extraordinary aquatic spaces.

In the following chapters, we will explore in detail how AI is transforming each stage of swimming pool construction. From design to maintenance, we will uncover the AI tools and techniques that are shaping the future of this industry. Join us on this exciting journey as we delve into the world of AI-driven innovation in swimming pool construction.

The transformation of the swimming pool industry with AI is not just a matter of improved tools but also a shift in the entire workflow and mindset. Traditional methods of pool construction often involved sequential stages, where delays in one phase could cascade and affect the entire project timeline. AI introduces the possibility of more integrated and parallel processes, significantly reducing the time from concept to completion.

The Integration of AI in Pool Construction

AI in Design

The design phase of pool construction is crucial, setting the foundation for the entire project. AI-driven design tools, such as parametric modeling software, have revolutionized this phase. These tools allow designers to input various parameters—such as site conditions, client preferences, and budget constraints—and generate optimized designs that meet all criteria. This not only speeds up the design process but also ensures a higher degree of customization and precision.

Furthermore, AI can enhance the visualization of pool designs.

Virtual reality (VR) and augmented reality (AR) technologies, powered by AI, offer clients an immersive experience of their future pool. They can virtually walk around the pool, make real-time adjustments, and see how changes will look, long before any physical work begins. This interactive approach reduces the likelihood of costly changes during the construction phase and increases client satisfaction.

AI in Excavation

Once the design is finalized, the excavation process begins. Traditionally, excavation is a labor-intensive and error-prone task. However, AI-powered machinery has transformed this aspect of construction. Autonomous excavators equipped with AI algorithms can analyze the terrain, calculate the optimal digging patterns, and execute the excavation with precision. These machines can adapt to unexpected obstacles, ensuring that the excavation is completed efficiently and accurately.

In addition to autonomous machinery, drones and LIDAR (Light Detection and Ranging) technology, guided by AI, provide detailed topographical data. This data helps in planning the excavation process and monitoring progress in real-time. The result is a significant reduction in excavation errors, leading to a smoother and faster construction process.

AI in Structural Engineering

Structural integrity is paramount in swimming pool construction. AI has brought a new level of precision to this critical aspect. Structural engineers use AI algorithms to analyze various factors, such as soil composition, load-bearing capacities, and environmental conditions, to determine the best materials and construction techniques. This ensures that the pool is not only aesthetically pleasing but also structurally sound and safe.

AI also plays a role in optimizing the use of materials. By analyzing historical data and current project parameters, AI can recommend the most efficient use of materials, reducing waste and lowering costs. This sustainable approach is increasingly important in today's construction industry, where environmental concerns are a top priority.

Smart Materials

The development of smart materials, facilitated by AI, has further enhanced the durability and functionality of swimming pools. These materials can respond to environmental changes, such as temperature fluctuations and chemical imbalances, ensuring the pool's longevity and reducing maintenance needs. For example, self-healing concrete, developed with the help of AI, can repair cracks automatically, preventing structural damage over time.

Nanotechnology, another area influenced by AI, has led to the creation of advanced coatings and finishes for pools. These coatings can repel dirt and algae, reducing the frequency of cleaning and maintenance. They can also enhance the aesthetic appeal of the pool by providing vibrant, long-lasting colors.

AI in Water Management

Water quality is a critical aspect of swimming pool operation. Traditional water management systems often require manual monitoring and adjustments, which can be time-consuming and prone to human error. AI-driven water management systems, on the other hand, can continuously monitor water quality parameters, such as pH levels, chlorine concentration, and temperature.

These systems use AI algorithms to analyze data in real-time and make automatic adjustments to maintain optimal water quality. They can also predict potential issues, such as chemical imbalances or equipment failures, and alert pool owners before problems arise. This proactive approach not only ensures a safe and enjoyable swimming experience but also extends the lifespan of pool equipment.

Sustainable Construction Practices

Sustainability is becoming a central focus in swimming pool construction, and AI is playing a pivotal role in promoting eco-friendly practices. AI can optimize energy consumption by controlling lighting, heating, and filtration systems based on usage patterns and environmental conditions. This reduces energy waste and lowers operational costs.

Recycled and sustainable materials are increasingly used in pool construction, and AI helps in selecting and sourcing these materials. For example, AI algorithms can analyze the environmental impact of different materials and recommend the most sustainable options. This not only reduces the carbon footprint of pool construction but also appeals to environmentally conscious consumers.

AI-Enhanced Safety Features

Safety is a paramount concern for pool owners, and AI has introduced innovative safety features that enhance the overall security of swimming pools. AI-powered sensors and monitoring systems can detect potential hazards, such as unattended children near the pool, water quality issues, or structural weaknesses. These systems provide real-time alerts, allowing pool owners to take immediate action and prevent accidents.

Additionally, AI can enhance the safety of pool construction sites. Autonomous machinery and AI-driven project management tools ensure that construction activities are conducted safely and efficiently. AI algorithms can analyze safety data and identify potential risks, enabling proactive measures to mitigate hazards.

AI in Maintenance

The role of AI extends beyond the construction phase to the maintenance of swimming pools. Traditional maintenance methods often involve periodic inspections and manual adjustments, which can be time-consuming and costly. AI-driven maintenance systems, on the other hand, continuously monitor the pool's condition and predict potential issues before they become major problems.

For example, AI algorithms can analyze data from sensors embedded in the pool structure to detect early signs of wear and tear. This allows for timely repairs, reducing the likelihood of costly damage and prolonging the life of the pool. Additionally, AI-driven maintenance systems can optimize the scheduling of routine tasks, such as cleaning and chemical balancing, ensuring that the pool remains in optimal condition with minimal effort.

Case Studies: Successful AI-Driven Pool Projects

To illustrate the transformative impact of AI in swimming pool construction, we will explore several case studies of successful AI-driven pool projects. These real-world examples demonstrate how AI technologies have been applied to create innovative and efficient pool designs, improve construction processes, and enhance overall pool performance.

Challenges and Limitations of AI in Pool Construction

Despite the numerous benefits, the integration of AI in swimming pool construction is not without challenges. Issues such as the high initial cost of AI technologies, the need for specialized skills and training, and concerns about data privacy and security must be addressed. This chapter will explore these challenges in detail and discuss potential solutions.

The Future Landscape of AI in Swimming Pools

The future of swimming pools lies in the seamless integration of AI technologies. As AI continues to evolve, we can expect even more advanced tools and techniques that will further enhance the efficiency, sustainability, and safety of pool construction and maintenance. This chapter will provide a glimpse into the future landscape of AI in swimming pools and explore emerging trends and innovations.

Embracing AI: Training and Skills Development for Pool Professionals

To fully realize the potential of AI in swimming pool construction, it is essential for pool professionals to embrace this technology and develop the necessary skills. This chapter will discuss the importance of training and education in AI for the pool construction industry. It will also provide resources and recommendations for professionals looking to enhance their AI expertise.

Conclusion

The integration of AI in swimming pool construction represents a significant leap forward for the industry. By enhancing design precision, optimizing construction processes, and improving maintenance and safety, AI is transforming the way swimming pools are built and maintained. As we continue to explore and embrace AI technologies, the future of swimming pools looks brighter and more innovative than ever before.

Chapter 2: Introduction to AI in Construction

The construction industry, one of the oldest and most traditional sectors, is undergoing a profound transformation thanks to the advent of artificial intelligence (AI). This chapter provides an in-depth introduction to AI in construction, exploring its origins, key technologies, and the potential it holds for revolutionizing the way we build.

The Origins of AI in Construction

Artificial intelligence, once the stuff of science fiction, has become a tangible reality in various industries, including construction. The origins of AI in construction can be traced back to the development of early computer-aided design (CAD) software and the increasing use of automation in construction processes. These initial steps laid the groundwork for more sophisticated AI applications that we see today.

The adoption of AI in construction gained momentum in the early 21st century, driven by advancements in machine learning, robotics, and data analytics. As these technologies matured, they began to be integrated into various aspects of construction, from design and planning to on-site operations and project management.

Key AI Technologies in Construction

Several key AI technologies are driving the transformation of the construction industry:

1. Machine Learning: Machine learning, a subset of AI, involves the use of algorithms that enable computers to learn from data and make predictions or decisions without explicit programming. In construction, machine learning algorithms analyze vast amounts of data from past projects to optimize planning, resource allocation, and risk management.

2. Computer Vision: Computer vision technology allows AI systems to interpret and understand visual information from the world. In construction, computer vision is used for tasks such as site monitoring, quality control, and safety inspections. Drones equipped with cameras and computer vision software can capture and analyze images of construction sites in real-time.

3. Robotics: Robotics is another crucial component of AI in construction. Autonomous and semi-autonomous robots can perform tasks such as bricklaying, concrete pouring, and excavation with precision and efficiency. These robots not only enhance productivity but also reduce the risk of accidents on construction sites.

4. Natural Language Processing (NLP): Natural language processing enables AI systems to understand and respond to human language. In construction, NLP is used for tasks such as project documentation, communication, and data extraction from textual sources. This technology improves collaboration and information management in construction projects.

5. Data Analytics: Data analytics involves analyzing large datasets to uncover patterns, trends, and insights that can inform decision-making. In construction, data analytics is used to optimize project schedules, manage costs, and improve quality control. By leveraging historical data, AI-driven analytics can predict potential issues and recommend proactive measures to mitigate risks.

The Benefits of AI in Construction

The integration of AI in construction brings numerous benefits, transforming the industry in several key areas:

1. Improved Efficiency: AI streamlines various construction processes, reducing the time and effort required to complete projects. Automated design tools, for example, can generate detailed blueprints quickly, while AI-powered machinery can perform tasks faster and with greater precision than human labor alone.

2. Enhanced Safety: Construction sites are inherently hazardous environments, with numerous potential risks to workers' safety. AI technologies, such as computer vision and robotics, help mitigate these risks by monitoring site conditions, detecting potential hazards, and automating dangerous tasks. This leads to a safer working environment and reduces the likelihood of accidents.

3. Cost Savings: AI-driven solutions can significantly reduce construction costs by optimizing resource allocation, minimizing waste, and improving project management. Predictive analytics, for instance, can identify potential delays or budget overruns early in the project, allowing for timely interventions that prevent cost escalation.

4. Better Quality Control: AI enhances quality control in construction by providing real-time monitoring and analysis of project activities. Computer vision technology can detect defects or deviations from design specifications, ensuring that issues are addressed promptly. This results in higher-quality construction and reduces the need for costly rework.

5. Sustainability: AI promotes sustainable construction practices by optimizing the use of materials and energy. AI algorithms can analyze the environmental impact of different construction methods and recommend the most sustainable options. Additionally, AI-driven systems can monitor and control energy consumption on construction sites, reducing the carbon footprint of projects.

Applications of AI in Swimming Pool Construction

The benefits of AI are particularly pronounced in the niche field of swimming pool construction. Here are some specific applications of AI in this context:

1. Customized Pool Design: AI-driven design tools allow for the creation of highly customized pool designs that cater to individual preferences and site conditions. By inputting various parameters, such as desired shape, size, and features, designers can generate optimized designs that meet the client's vision and requirements.

2. Precision Excavation: Autonomous excavators and drones equipped with AI can perform excavation tasks with high precision, reducing the risk of errors and minimizing environmental impact. This technology ensures that the pool's foundation is excavated accurately, setting the stage for a smooth construction process.

3. Structural Analysis: AI algorithms assist structural engineers in analyzing various factors that affect the pool's integrity, such as soil composition, load-bearing capacities, and environmental conditions. This ensures that the pool is constructed with the best materials and techniques, enhancing its durability and safety.

4. Smart Materials: AI has facilitated the development of smart materials that offer superior performance in swimming pool construction. These materials can adapt to changing conditions, such as water chemistry and temperature, ensuring the longevity and safety of the pool. Examples include self-healing concrete and advanced coatings that repel dirt and algae.

5. Automated Water Management: AI-driven water management systems continuously monitor water quality parameters and make automatic adjustments to maintain optimal conditions. These systems reduce the need for manual interventions and chemical treatments, promoting a healthier swimming environment and reducing maintenance efforts.

6. Sustainable Practices: AI promotes sustainable practices in pool construction by optimizing the use of recycled and eco-friendly materials. AI algorithms analyze the environmental impact of different materials and construction methods, recommending the most sustainable options. Additionally, AI-driven systems optimize energy consumption for pool lighting, heating, and filtration, reducing the overall environmental footprint.

Overcoming Challenges in AI Adoption

Despite the numerous benefits, the adoption of AI in swimming pool construction is not without challenges. Addressing these challenges is crucial to fully realize the potential of AI in the industry:

1. High Initial Costs: Implementing AI technologies often requires significant upfront investment in software, hardware, and training. To overcome this barrier, construction companies can explore financing options, government grants, and partnerships with technology providers to make AI adoption more affordable.

2. Skill Development: The integration of AI in construction requires a workforce skilled in using and maintaining AI technologies. Training programs and continuous education are essential to equip construction professionals with the necessary skills. Collaborations with educational institutions and industry associations can help bridge the skills gap.

3. Data Privacy and Security: The use of AI involves the collection and analysis of large amounts of data, raising concerns about data privacy and security. Construction companies must implement robust data protection measures and comply with relevant regulations to ensure the confidentiality and integrity of project data.

4. Resistance to Change: Like any industry, the construction sector can be resistant to change. Overcoming this resistance requires clear communication of the benefits of AI, demonstration of successful AI-driven projects, and involvement of all stakeholders in the transition process. Building a culture that embraces innovation is key to successful AI adoption.

5. Integration with Existing Systems: Integrating AI technologies with existing construction systems and processes can be challenging. A phased approach to implementation, starting with pilot projects and gradually scaling up, can help ensure a smooth transition. Additionally, working with technology partners who offer comprehensive integration support can facilitate this process.

Conclusion

The integration of AI in swimming pool construction represents a significant leap forward for the industry. By enhancing design precision, optimizing construction processes, and improving maintenance and safety, AI is transforming the way swimming pools are built and maintained. As we continue to explore and embrace AI technologies, the future of swimming pools looks brighter and more innovative than ever before.

Chapter 3: AI Tools
Revolutionizing Pool Design

The design phase of swimming pool construction is critical, as it sets the foundation for the entire project. AI-driven tools are revolutionizing this phase, enabling designers to create intricate, customized, and efficient pool designs that meet the diverse needs and preferences of clients. This chapter delves into the various AI tools that are transforming pool design and explores their applications and benefits.

AI-Driven Design Software

One of the most significant advancements in pool design is the development of AI-driven design software. These tools leverage machine learning algorithms and parametric modeling to generate optimized designs based on various input parameters.

1. Parametric Modeling: Parametric modeling allows designers to create complex pool designs by defining parameters and relationships between different design elements. AI algorithms analyze these parameters and generate multiple design iterations, ensuring that the final design meets all specified criteria. This approach enables designers to explore a wide range of design possibilities quickly and efficiently.

2. Generative Design: Generative design is an AI-driven process where the software generates numerous design options based on defined constraints and goals. Designers input parameters such as site conditions, budget, and aesthetic preferences, and the AI generates a range of design solutions. This not only accelerates the design process but also ensures that the final design is optimized for performance, aesthetics, and cost.

3. 3D Visualization: AI-powered 3D visualization tools provide clients with an immersive experience of their future pool. Virtual reality (VR) and augmented reality (AR) technologies enable clients to explore the pool design in a virtual environment, making real-time adjustments and seeing how changes will look. This interactive approach enhances client engagement and satisfaction, reducing the likelihood of costly changes during construction.

AI in Site Analysis and Planning

AI tools are also transforming site analysis and planning, ensuring that pool designs are not only aesthetically pleasing but also feasible and sustainable.

1. Site Analysis: AI algorithms analyze various site-specific factors, such as topography, soil composition, and climate conditions, to inform the pool design. By leveraging data from drones, LIDAR, and geographic information systems (GIS), AI tools provide detailed insights into site conditions, enabling designers to create designs that are well-suited to the environment.

2. Environmental Impact Assessment: AI-driven tools assess the environmental impact of different design options, helping designers choose sustainable materials and construction methods. These tools analyze factors such as energy consumption, water usage, and carbon footprint, promoting eco-friendly pool designs that minimize environmental impact.

3. Resource Optimization: AI tools optimize the use of resources, such as materials and labor, during the design phase. By analyzing historical data and current project parameters, AI algorithms recommend the most efficient use of resources, reducing waste and lowering costs. This sustainable approach is increasingly important in today's construction industry, where environmental concerns are a top priority.

Customization and Personalization

One of the most significant advantages of AI-driven design tools is their ability to deliver highly customized and personalized pool designs.

1. Personalized Recommendations: AI algorithms analyze client preferences, lifestyle, and usage patterns to provide personalized design recommendations. For example, if a client frequently hosts pool parties, the AI might suggest incorporating features such as a larger deck area, built-in seating, and advanced lighting systems. This level of personalization ensures that the final design meets the unique needs and preferences of each client.

2. Real-Time Adjustments: AI-driven design tools allow for real-time adjustments during the design phase. Clients can experiment with different design elements, such as shapes, materials, and features, and see the impact of these changes instantly. This interactive approach enhances client satisfaction and ensures that the final design aligns with their vision.

3. Budget Optimization: AI tools help optimize the design to fit within the client's budget. By analyzing cost data from past projects and current market conditions, AI algorithms recommend design modifications that reduce costs without compromising quality or aesthetics. This ensures that clients receive a high-quality pool that meets their budget constraints.

Case Studies: AI-Driven Pool Designs

To illustrate the transformative impact of AI-driven design tools, this chapter will present several case studies of successful AI-driven pool designs. These real-world examples demonstrate how AI technologies have been applied to create innovative, efficient, and personalized pool designs that meet the diverse needs of clients.

Conclusion

AI-driven design tools are revolutionizing the pool design phase, enabling designers to create intricate, customized, and efficient designs that meet the diverse needs and preferences of clients. By leveraging advanced technologies such as parametric modeling, generative design, and 3D visualization, designers can deliver high-quality, personalized pool designs quickly and efficiently. As AI continues to evolve, we can expect even more advanced tools and techniques that will further enhance the pool design process, making it more innovative, efficient, and client-centric.

Chapter 4: AI in Pool Excavation and Structural Engineering

The excavation and structural engineering phases of swimming pool construction are critical to ensuring the pool's stability, safety, and longevity. AI technologies are transforming these phases, enhancing precision, efficiency, and sustainability. This chapter explores the various AI applications in pool excavation and structural engineering, highlighting their benefits and impact on the industry.

AI-Driven Excavation

Excavation is a labor-intensive and error-prone task that requires precision and expertise. AI-powered machinery and technologies have revolutionized this aspect of construction, making the excavation process more efficient and accurate.

1. Autonomous Excavators: Autonomous excavators equipped with AI algorithms can analyze the terrain, calculate optimal digging patterns, and execute the excavation with high precision. These machines adapt to unexpected obstacles and ensure that the excavation is completed efficiently and accurately. This reduces the risk of errors and minimizes environmental impact.

2. Drones and LIDAR: Drones equipped with cameras and LIDAR technology, guided by AI, provide detailed topographical data of the excavation site. This data helps in planning the excavation process and monitoring progress in real-time. AI algorithms analyze the data to identify potential issues, such as uneven terrain or hidden obstacles, ensuring a smooth and efficient excavation process.

3. Real-Time Monitoring: AI-driven excavation systems offer real-time monitoring and feedback, allowing for immediate adjustments and corrections. Sensors embedded in the excavation equipment collect data on factors such as soil stability, equipment performance, and excavation depth. AI algorithms analyze this data and provide real-time insights, ensuring that the excavation is progressing according to plan.

AI in Structural Engineering

Structural engineering is critical to ensuring the stability and safety of swimming pools. AI technologies enhance this phase by providing advanced analysis and optimization tools.

1. Structural Analysis: AI algorithms assist structural engineers in analyzing various factors that affect the pool's stability, such as soil composition, load-bearing capacities, and environmental conditions. This ensures that the pool is constructed with the best materials and techniques, enhancing its durability and safety.

2. Material Optimization: AI tools optimize the use of materials in pool construction, reducing waste and lowering costs. By analyzing data from past projects and current project parameters, AI algorithms recommend the most efficient use of materials, ensuring that the pool is built sustainably and economically.

3. Simulation and Testing: AI-driven simulation tools allow engineers to test different structural designs and materials virtually before construction begins. These simulations provide insights into how the pool will perform under various conditions, such as heavy usage, extreme weather, and soil movement. This proactive approach reduces the risk of structural failures and ensures that the pool is built to withstand the test of time.

4. Smart Materials: The development of smart materials, facilitated by AI, has further enhanced the durability and functionality of swimming pools. These materials can respond to environmental changes, such as temperature fluctuations and chemical imbalances, ensuring the pool's longevity and reducing maintenance needs. For example, self-healing concrete, developed with the help of AI, can repair cracks automatically, preventing structural damage over time.

Case Studies: AI-Driven Excavation and Structural Engineering

To illustrate the transformative impact of AI in pool excavation and structural engineering, this chapter will present several case studies of successful AI-driven projects. These real-world examples demonstrate how AI technologies have been applied to enhance precision, efficiency, and sustainability in these critical phases of pool construction.

Challenges and Solutions in AI-Driven Excavation and Engineering

Despite the numerous benefits, the integration of AI in excavation and structural engineering comes with its own set of challenges. Addressing these challenges is crucial to fully realizing the potential of AI in these phases:

1. **High Initial Investment:** Implementing AI technologies in excavation and structural engineering often requires significant upfront investment in equipment, software, and training. To overcome this barrier, construction companies can explore financing options, government grants, and partnerships with technology providers to make AI adoption more affordable.

2. **Skill Development:** The integration of AI requires a workforce skilled in using and maintaining AI technologies. Training programs and continuous education are essential to equip construction professionals with the necessary skills. Collaborations with educational institutions and industry associations can help bridge the skills gap.

3. **Data Privacy and Security:** The use of AI involves the collection

and analysis of large amounts of data, raising concerns about data privacy and security. Construction companies must implement robust data protection measures and comply with relevant regulations to ensure the confidentiality and integrity of project data.

4. Resistance to Change: Like any industry, the construction sector can be resistant to change. Overcoming this resistance requires clear communication of the benefits of AI, demonstration of successful AI-driven projects, and involvement of all stakeholders in the transition process. Building a culture that embraces innovation is key to successful AI adoption.

Conclusion

The integration of AI in pool excavation and structural engineering represents a significant advancement for the industry. By enhancing precision, efficiency, and sustainability, AI is transforming the way swimming pools are built. As we continue to explore and embrace AI technologies, the future of swimming pool construction looks brighter and more innovative than ever before.

Chapter 5: AI-Enhanced Water Management Systems

Water quality is a critical aspect of swimming pool operation, directly impacting the safety and enjoyment of pool users. Traditional water management systems often require manual monitoring and adjustments, which can be time-consuming and prone to human error. AI-driven water management systems are revolutionizing this aspect of pool maintenance, offering real-time monitoring, predictive analytics, and automated adjustments to ensure optimal water quality.

AI-Driven Monitoring and Control Systems

AI-driven water management systems continuously monitor various water quality parameters, such as pH levels, chlorine concentration, temperature, and turbidity. These systems use AI algorithms to analyze data in real-time and make automatic adjustments to maintain optimal water quality.

1. Real-Time Monitoring: Sensors embedded in the pool structure and filtration system collect data on water quality parameters. AI algorithms analyze this data in real-time, providing continuous monitoring and immediate alerts if any parameter deviates from the desired range. This proactive approach ensures that water quality issues are detected and addressed promptly.

2. Predictive Analytics: AI-driven water management systems use predictive analytics to forecast potential water quality issues before they arise. By analyzing historical data and identifying patterns, these systems can predict when certain parameters are likely to deviate from the norm and take preventive measures. For example, if the system detects that pH levels tend to drop after heavy pool usage, it can automatically adjust chemical dosing to prevent imbalances.

3. Automated Adjustments: AI algorithms enable water management systems to make automatic adjustments to maintain optimal water quality. This includes adjusting chemical dosing, filtration cycles, and water circulation based on real-time data. Automated adjustments reduce the need for manual interventions and ensure consistent water quality, enhancing the safety and enjoyment of pool users.

Advanced Filtration Systems

AI technologies have also led to the development of advanced filtration systems that offer superior performance and efficiency.

1. Smart Filters: Smart filters equipped with AI sensors monitor the condition of the filtration media and optimize the filtration process. These filters can detect when the media is becoming clogged and automatically initiate backwashing or replacement cycles. This ensures that the filtration system operates at peak efficiency, maintaining optimal water clarity and quality.

2. Energy Efficiency: AI-driven filtration systems optimize energy consumption by adjusting filtration cycles based on usage patterns and environmental conditions. For example, the system can reduce filtration intensity during periods of low pool usage and increase it during peak times. This approach not only maintains water quality but also reduces energy costs and promotes sustainability.

Chemical Management

Proper chemical balance is essential for maintaining safe and clean pool water. AI-driven chemical management systems automate the dosing and monitoring of pool chemicals, ensuring precise and consistent levels.

1. Automated Dosing: AI algorithms analyze real-time data on water quality parameters and calculate the precise amount of chemicals needed to maintain optimal balance. Automated dosing systems then dispense the required chemicals, ensuring consistent levels and reducing the risk of over- or under-dosing. This enhances water safety and reduces chemical wastage.

2. Chemical Usage Optimization: AI-driven systems optimize chemical usage by predicting demand and adjusting dosing schedules accordingly. For example, the system can increase chlorine dosing during periods of high pool usage to maintain sanitation and reduce it during low usage periods. This not only ensures water quality but also minimizes chemical consumption and costs.

AI-Enhanced Safety Features

AI-driven water management systems offer advanced safety features that enhance the overall security of swimming pools.

1. Remote Monitoring and Control: AI systems enable remote monitoring and control of pool water quality through mobile apps and web interfaces. Pool owners and operators can access real-time data, receive alerts, and make adjustments from anywhere, ensuring that water quality is always maintained. This remote capability enhances convenience and ensures timely interventions in case of issues.

2. Leak Detection: AI-driven systems can detect leaks in the pool structure and plumbing by analyzing data on water levels and usage patterns. Early detection of leaks allows for prompt repairs, preventing water loss and structural damage. This enhances the safety and longevity of the pool.

Case Studies: AI-Enhanced Water Management

To illustrate the impact of AI-driven water management systems, this chapter will present several case studies of successful implementations. These real-world examples demonstrate how AI technologies have been applied to maintain optimal water quality, enhance safety, and reduce maintenance efforts in swimming pools.

Overcoming Challenges in AI-Enhanced Water Management

The adoption of AI-driven water management systems comes with its own set of challenges. Addressing these challenges is crucial to fully realizing the benefits of AI in pool maintenance:

1. **High Initial Costs:** Implementing AI-driven water management systems often requires significant upfront investment in sensors, software, and training. To overcome this barrier, pool owners and operators can explore financing options, government grants, and partnerships with technology providers to make AI adoption more affordable.

2. **Skill Development:** The integration of AI requires a workforce skilled in using and maintaining AI technologies. Training programs and continuous education are essential to equip pool maintenance professionals with the necessary skills. Collaborations with educational institutions and industry associations can help bridge the skills gap.

3. **Data Privacy and Security:** The use of AI involves the collection and analysis of large amounts of data, raising concerns about data privacy and security. Pool owners and operators must implement robust data protection measures and comply with relevant regulations to ensure the confidentiality and integrity of water quality data.

4. **Resistance to Change:** Like any industry, the pool

maintenance sector can be resistant to change. Overcoming this resistance requires clear communication of the benefits of AI, demonstration of successful AI-driven projects, and involvement of all stakeholders in the transition process. Building a culture that embraces innovation is key to successful AI adoption.

Conclusion

AI-enhanced water management systems represent a significant advancement in swimming pool maintenance. By providing real-time monitoring, predictive analytics, and automated adjustments, these systems ensure optimal water quality and enhance the safety and enjoyment of pool users. As we continue to explore and embrace AI technologies, the future of swimming pool maintenance looks brighter and more innovative than ever before.

Chapter 6: The Future of AI in Swimming Pool Construction

The integration of AI in swimming pool construction has already brought significant advancements, but the potential for future developments is even more exciting. This chapter explores the future trends and innovations that will shape the swimming pool construction industry, driven by AI technologies.

AI and IoT Integration

The Internet of Things (IoT) is set to play a crucial role in the future of AI-driven swimming pool construction. The integration of AI and IoT will enable even more advanced monitoring, control, and automation of pool systems.

1. Smart Pool Ecosystems: AI and IoT will create smart pool ecosystems where all pool components, such as pumps, filters, heaters, and lighting, are interconnected and controlled by AI algorithms. This seamless integration will allow for holistic management of the pool, optimizing performance and efficiency across all systems.

2. Enhanced User Experience: Smart pool ecosystems will enhance the user experience by providing personalized settings and recommendations. For example, AI algorithms can learn users' preferences for water temperature, lighting, and filtration schedules, automatically adjusting the pool environment to meet their needs. This level of customization will make pool ownership more enjoyable and convenient.

Advanced Robotics in Construction

The future of AI in swimming pool construction will see even greater use of advanced robotics. These robots will perform a wide range of tasks with high precision and efficiency.

1. Autonomous Construction Robots: Autonomous robots equipped with AI will handle various construction tasks, such as excavation, material handling, and structural assembly. These robots will work collaboratively, communicating with each other and AI-driven control systems to ensure seamless construction processes.

2. 3D Printing Technology: AI-driven 3D printing technology will revolutionize pool construction by enabling the creation of complex, custom-designed pool components on-site. This approach will reduce construction time, minimize material waste, and allow for more innovative and personalized pool designs.

AI-Driven Sustainability

Sustainability will be a key focus of future AI developments in swimming pool construction. AI technologies will continue to promote eco-friendly practices and optimize resource usage.

1. Green Building Materials: AI algorithms will help identify and develop new green building materials that offer superior performance and sustainability. These materials will reduce the environmental impact of pool construction and enhance the durability and longevity of the pool.

2. Energy Management: AI-driven energy management systems will optimize the use of renewable energy sources, such as solar and geothermal, for pool heating and lighting. These systems will ensure that pools operate efficiently and sustainably, reducing energy costs and environmental impact.

Predictive Maintenance and AI

Predictive maintenance, powered by AI, will become even more sophisticated, ensuring that swimming pools are always in optimal condition.

1. Advanced Predictive Analytics: AI algorithms will analyze data from various pool components to predict potential issues before they occur. This proactive approach will allow for timely maintenance and repairs, minimizing downtime and extending the lifespan of the pool.

2. Self-Healing Systems: AI-driven self-healing systems will detect and repair minor issues automatically, such as small cracks or leaks. These systems will use advanced materials and technologies to address problems before they escalate, ensuring the long-term durability and safety of the pool.

AI-Enhanced User Interfaces

The user interfaces of AI-driven pool systems will become more intuitive and user-friendly, enhancing the overall experience for pool owners and operators.

1. Voice-Activated Controls: AI-driven voice-activated controls will allow users to manage their pool systems through simple voice commands. This hands-free approach will enhance convenience and make it easier for users to interact with their pool systems.

2. Augmented Reality Interfaces: Augmented reality (AR) interfaces will provide users with a visual representation of their pool systems, making it easier to understand and manage various components. AR technology will offer real-time data visualization and interactive controls, enhancing the overall user experience.

Conclusion

The future of AI in swimming pool construction is filled with exciting possibilities. The integration of AI and IoT, advanced robotics, sustainability, predictive maintenance, and enhanced user interfaces will continue to transform the industry, making pool construction more innovative, efficient, and user-centric. As we embrace these advancements, the swimming pool construction industry will continue to evolve, offering even greater benefits and opportunities for pool owners and operators.

Chapter 7: AI in Pool Heating and Energy Efficiency

As energy costs rise and environmental concerns become more prominent, the need for efficient and sustainable pool heating solutions is greater than ever. AI technologies are revolutionizing pool heating systems, optimizing energy use, and improving overall efficiency. This chapter delves into how AI is enhancing pool heating and promoting energy efficiency, ensuring pools remain comfortable and eco-friendly.

AI-Driven Pool Heating Systems

AI-driven pool heating systems utilize advanced algorithms to monitor and control the heating process, ensuring optimal temperature management with minimal energy consumption.

1. Smart Thermostats: AI-powered smart thermostats analyze weather forecasts, pool usage patterns, and historical data to predict and maintain the ideal pool temperature. These systems automatically adjust heating schedules to match user preferences and environmental conditions, optimizing energy use and reducing costs.

2. Predictive Heating: Predictive heating systems use AI to anticipate when the pool will be used and preheat it accordingly. By learning user habits and integrating with smart home systems, these heating solutions ensure the pool is always ready for use while minimizing energy waste.

3. Solar Integration: AI systems can optimize the use of solar energy for pool heating, adjusting heating schedules based on solar panel output and weather conditions. This approach maximizes the utilization of renewable energy, reducing reliance on traditional heating methods and lowering carbon footprints.

Energy Efficiency and AI

AI technologies are significantly enhancing the energy efficiency of swimming pools, reducing operational costs and environmental impact.

1. Energy Consumption Monitoring: AI-driven systems continuously monitor energy consumption across all pool components, identifying inefficiencies and optimizing performance. These systems provide detailed insights into energy usage, helping pool owners make informed decisions to enhance efficiency.

2. Load Balancing: AI algorithms balance the load on pool heating systems, distributing energy consumption more evenly and preventing peak usage spikes. This reduces strain on the electrical grid and ensures a more stable and efficient energy supply.

3. Demand Response: AI systems can participate in demand response programs, adjusting pool heating and other energy-intensive operations during peak demand periods. This helps reduce overall energy consumption and lowers costs by taking advantage of off-peak rates.

Case Studies: AI in Pool Heating and Energy Efficiency

This section will showcase several case studies demonstrating the successful implementation of AI-driven pool heating and energy efficiency solutions. These real-world examples highlight the benefits of AI technologies in reducing energy consumption, lowering costs, and promoting sustainability.

Overcoming Challenges in AI-Enhanced Heating and Efficiency

While AI-driven pool heating and energy efficiency systems offer numerous benefits, there are challenges that must be addressed to ensure successful implementation.

1. Initial Investment: The upfront costs of installing AI-driven heating and energy efficiency systems can be high. Pool owners can explore financing options, government incentives, and partnerships with technology providers to make these solutions more accessible.

2. Integration with Existing Systems: Integrating AI technologies with existing pool systems can be complex. To overcome this, pool owners should work with experienced professionals who can ensure seamless integration and compatibility.

3. Data Management: Effective data management is crucial for AI-driven systems. Pool owners must ensure that their systems are capable of handling and processing large volumes of data, maintaining accuracy and reliability.

4. User Training: Proper training is essential for pool owners and operators to fully utilize AI-driven heating and energy efficiency systems. Comprehensive training programs and ongoing support can help users maximize the benefits of these advanced technologies.

Conclusion

AI-driven pool heating and energy efficiency solutions are transforming the way swimming pools are heated and maintained. By optimizing energy use, reducing costs, and promoting sustainability, these technologies ensure that pools remain comfortable and eco-friendly. As we continue to explore and embrace AI advancements, the future of pool heating and energy efficiency looks brighter and more innovative than ever before.

Chapter 8: AI in Pool Safety and Security

Ensuring the safety and security of swimming pools is paramount for pool owners and operators. AI technologies are enhancing pool safety and security measures, providing advanced monitoring, detection, and response capabilities. This chapter explores how AI is revolutionizing pool safety and security, protecting pool users and property.

AI-Enhanced Pool Safety Systems

AI-driven safety systems utilize advanced algorithms and sensors to monitor pool environments, detect potential hazards, and respond promptly to ensure user safety.

1. Drowning Detection: AI-powered drowning detection systems use cameras and sensors to monitor pool activity in real-time. These systems analyze movement patterns and can distinguish between normal swimming behavior and potential drowning incidents. When a threat is detected, the system immediately alerts pool staff or emergency services, enabling a swift response.

2. Slip and Fall Prevention: AI systems can identify areas around the pool where slip and fall incidents are likely to occur. By analyzing factors such as surface conditions, weather, and user behavior, these systems can provide warnings and recommendations to mitigate risks. For example, AI algorithms can suggest the application of anti-slip coatings or adjustments to poolside design to enhance safety.

3. Hazardous Chemical Detection: AI-driven sensors continuously monitor pool water for hazardous chemical levels. If the system detects abnormal levels of chemicals such as chlorine or pH imbalances, it can automatically adjust chemical dosing or alert maintenance personnel to take corrective action. This ensures a safe swimming environment and prevents chemical-related accidents.

AI-Enhanced Pool Security Systems

AI technologies are also enhancing pool security measures, protecting against unauthorized access and ensuring the safety of pool users.

1. Access Control: AI-powered access control systems use facial recognition, biometric data, and smart locks to ensure that only authorized individuals can access the pool area. These systems can also integrate with smart home devices, providing seamless and secure access for pool owners and their guests.

2. Perimeter Surveillance: AI-driven surveillance cameras monitor the pool perimeter, detecting and alerting security personnel to any suspicious activity. These systems use advanced image recognition algorithms to identify potential threats, such as intruders or vandalism, and can trigger alarms or notifications to ensure a rapid response.

3. Smart Lighting: AI-enhanced smart lighting systems can automatically adjust poolside lighting based on activity and environmental conditions. For example, these systems can increase lighting intensity during nighttime swimming sessions or dim lights when the pool is not in use, enhancing both safety and energy efficiency.

Case Studies: AI in Pool Safety and Security

This section will present several case studies highlighting the successful implementation of AI-driven pool safety and security systems. These real-world examples demonstrate how AI technologies have enhanced safety and security measures, protecting pool users and property.

Overcoming Challenges in AI-Enhanced Safety and Security

Implementing AI-driven pool safety and security systems comes with its own set of challenges. Addressing these challenges is crucial to fully realize the benefits of AI in pool safety and security:

1. **Privacy Concerns:** AI-driven surveillance and monitoring systems raise privacy concerns. Pool owners must ensure that these systems comply with privacy regulations and implement measures to protect user data, such as data encryption and access controls.

2. **System Reliability:** The reliability of AI-driven safety and security systems is critical. Pool owners should choose systems with robust backup and failover mechanisms to ensure continuous operation even in the event of a system failure.

3. **Cost:** The cost of implementing advanced AI-driven safety and security systems can be high. Exploring financing options, government grants, and partnerships with technology providers can help make these systems more affordable.

4. **User Training:** Proper training is essential for pool owners and operators to effectively use AI-driven safety and security systems. Comprehensive training programs and ongoing support can help users maximize the benefits of these advanced technologies.

Conclusion

AI-driven safety and security systems are revolutionizing the way swimming pools are monitored and protected. By providing advanced detection, monitoring, and response capabilities, these technologies ensure the safety and security of pool users and property. As we continue to explore and embrace AI advancements, the future of pool safety and security looks brighter and more innovative than ever before.

Chapter 9: AI in Pool Cleaning and Maintenance

Maintaining a clean and well-functioning swimming pool requires regular cleaning and maintenance. AI technologies are transforming pool cleaning and maintenance processes, offering advanced automation, predictive maintenance, and efficient resource management. This chapter delves into how AI is enhancing pool cleaning and maintenance, ensuring pools remain pristine and well-maintained.

AI-Driven Pool Cleaning Systems

AI-powered pool cleaning systems utilize advanced algorithms and sensors to automate and optimize the cleaning process, ensuring thorough and efficient maintenance.

1. Robotic Pool Cleaners: Robotic pool cleaners equipped with AI algorithms can navigate and clean the pool autonomously. These robots use sensors to detect debris, algae, and other contaminants, adjusting their cleaning patterns to ensure complete coverage. AI algorithms optimize cleaning routes, reducing cleaning time and energy consumption.

2. Smart Filtration Systems: AI-driven smart filtration systems continuously monitor water quality and adjust filtration cycles accordingly. These systems use sensors to detect changes in water clarity, temperature, and chemical levels, optimizing filtration efficiency and ensuring that the pool remains clean and safe.

3. Self-Cleaning Surfaces: Innovative self-cleaning pool surfaces, developed with the help of AI, repel dirt and contaminants, reducing the need for manual cleaning. These surfaces use advanced materials and nanotechnology to minimize the buildup of algae and other debris, ensuring a cleaner pool with less maintenance effort.

Predictive Maintenance and AI

Predictive maintenance, powered by AI, ensures that pool equipment and systems are maintained proactively, preventing issues before they occur and extending the lifespan of pool components.

1. Equipment Monitoring: AI-driven systems continuously monitor the condition of pool equipment, such as pumps, filters, and heaters. By analyzing data from sensors and identifying patterns, these systems can predict when maintenance or repairs are needed, ensuring that equipment operates efficiently and reducing the risk of unexpected failures.

2. Maintenance Scheduling: AI algorithms can optimize maintenance schedules based on usage patterns, equipment condition, and environmental factors. This proactive approach ensures that maintenance tasks are performed at the optimal time, minimizing downtime and extending the lifespan of pool components.

3. Resource Management: AI-driven resource management systems optimize the use of chemicals, water, and energy in pool maintenance. These systems ensure that resources are used efficiently, reducing waste and lowering operational costs.

Case Studies: AI in Pool Cleaning and Maintenance

This section will showcase several case studies demonstrating the successful implementation of AI-driven pool cleaning and maintenance solutions. These real-world examples highlight the benefits of AI technologies in maintaining clean and well-functioning swimming pools.

Overcoming Challenges in AI-Enhanced Cleaning and Maintenance

Implementing AI-driven pool cleaning and maintenance systems comes with its own set of challenges. Addressing these challenges is crucial to fully realize the benefits of AI in pool maintenance:

1. Initial Investment: The upfront costs of installing AI-driven cleaning and maintenance systems can be high. Pool owners can explore financing options, government incentives, and partnerships with technology providers to make these solutions more accessible.

2. Integration with Existing Systems: Integrating AI technologies with existing pool systems can be complex. Pool owners should work with experienced professionals to ensure seamless integration and compatibility.

3. Data Management: Effective data management is essential for AI-driven systems. Pool owners must ensure that their systems are capable of handling and processing large volumes of data, maintaining accuracy and reliability.

4. User Training: Proper training is essential for pool owners and operators to fully utilize AI-driven cleaning and maintenance systems. Comprehensive training programs and ongoing support can help users maximize the benefits of these advanced technologies.

Conclusion

AI-driven pool cleaning and maintenance solutions are transforming the way swimming pools are maintained. By automating and optimizing cleaning processes, predicting maintenance needs, and managing resources efficiently, these technologies ensure that pools remain pristine and well-maintained. As we continue to explore and embrace AI advancements, the future of pool cleaning and maintenance looks brighter and more innovative than ever before.

Chapter 10: AI in Pool Design and Customization

AI technologies are revolutionizing the design and customization of swimming pools, offering innovative solutions that enhance aesthetics, functionality, and user experience. This chapter explores how AI is transforming pool design and customization, providing advanced tools and capabilities for creating unique and personalized pools.

AI-Enhanced Pool Design Tools

AI-driven design tools enable pool designers and architects to create stunning and functional pool designs with greater efficiency and precision.

1. 3D Modeling and Visualization: AI-powered 3D modeling and visualization tools allow designers to create detailed and accurate representations of pool designs. These tools use AI algorithms to generate realistic renderings, enabling clients to visualize their pool before construction begins and make informed design decisions.

2. Custom Design Recommendations: AI algorithms analyze client preferences, site conditions, and design trends to provide custom design recommendations. These systems can suggest design elements, materials, and features that align with the client's vision and enhance the overall aesthetic and functionality of the pool.

3. Environmental Analysis: AI-driven environmental analysis tools assess factors such as sun exposure, wind patterns, and topography to optimize pool design. These tools ensure that the pool is positioned and designed to maximize comfort, energy efficiency, and overall enjoyment.

Personalized Pool Features

AI technologies enable the creation of personalized pool features that cater to individual preferences and enhance the user experience.

1. Adaptive Lighting: AI-driven adaptive lighting systems adjust pool lighting based on user preferences, time of day, and activity. These systems can create dynamic lighting effects, such as color-changing lights for evening parties or soft ambient lighting for relaxation, enhancing the overall pool experience.

2. Custom Water Features: AI algorithms can design and control custom water features, such as fountains, waterfalls, and jets. These features can be programmed to create unique patterns and effects, providing a personalized and visually stunning pool environment.

3. Temperature Control: AI-powered temperature control systems ensure that the pool water temperature is always comfortable for users. These systems can learn user preferences and adjust heating or cooling schedules accordingly, providing a tailored and enjoyable swimming experience.

Case Studies: AI in Pool Design and Customization

This section will showcase several case studies demonstrating the successful implementation of AI-driven pool design and customization solutions. These real-world examples highlight the benefits of AI technologies in creating unique and personalized pools.

Overcoming Challenges in AI-Enhanced Design and Customization

Implementing AI-driven pool design and customization systems comes with its own set of challenges. Addressing these challenges is crucial to fully realize the benefits of AI in pool design:

1. Design Complexity: AI-driven design tools can be complex and require specialized knowledge. Pool designers and architects should invest in training and professional development to effectively use these advanced tools.

2. Integration with Construction: Integrating AI-driven design solutions with the construction process can be challenging. Ensuring seamless communication and collaboration between designers, architects, and construction teams is essential for successful implementation.

3. Cost: The cost of implementing advanced AI-driven design and customization systems can be high. Exploring financing options, government incentives, and partnerships with technology providers can help make these solutions more accessible.

4. Client Education: Educating clients about the benefits and capabilities of AI-driven design and customization is crucial. Providing detailed information and demonstrations can help clients understand and appreciate the value of these advanced technologies.

Conclusion

AI-driven pool design and customization solutions are transforming the way swimming pools are designed and personalized. By offering advanced design tools, personalized features, and environmental analysis, these technologies enhance the aesthetics, functionality, and user experience of pools. As we continue to explore and embrace AI advancements, the future of pool design and customization looks brighter and more innovative than ever before.

Chapter 11: AI in Pool Operations and Management

Efficient and effective pool operations and management are crucial for ensuring a positive experience for pool users and maintaining optimal pool conditions. AI technologies are enhancing pool operations and management, offering advanced tools and capabilities for optimizing performance, resource management, and user satisfaction. This chapter explores how AI is transforming pool operations and management, providing innovative solutions for pool owners and operators.

AI-Driven Pool Operations Management

AI-powered management systems provide pool owners and operators with advanced tools for optimizing pool operations and ensuring smooth and efficient management.

1. Operational Efficiency: AI-driven systems analyze data from various pool components, such as pumps, filters, heaters, and lighting, to optimize operational efficiency. These systems can identify inefficiencies, recommend adjustments, and automate processes, reducing energy consumption and operational costs.

2. Real-Time Monitoring: AI-powered real-time monitoring systems continuously track pool conditions, such as water quality, temperature, and chemical levels. These systems provide instant alerts and recommendations, ensuring that pool conditions are always optimal and enabling prompt corrective actions when needed.

3. Automated Scheduling: AI algorithms can optimize scheduling for various pool operations, such as cleaning, maintenance, and heating. By analyzing usage patterns and environmental factors, these systems ensure that operations are performed at the most efficient times, minimizing disruptions and maximizing efficiency.

Resource Management and AI

AI technologies are enhancing resource management for swimming pools, ensuring efficient use of water, chemicals, and energy.

1. Water Conservation: AI-driven water management systems optimize water usage by monitoring and adjusting water levels, detecting leaks, and minimizing evaporation. These systems ensure that pools operate efficiently while conserving water resources.

2. Chemical Management: AI-powered chemical management systems continuously monitor water quality and adjust chemical dosing to maintain optimal levels. These systems reduce chemical waste and ensure safe and balanced water conditions, enhancing user safety and comfort.

3. Energy Optimization: AI-driven energy management systems optimize the use of energy for heating, lighting, and other pool operations. By analyzing energy consumption patterns and environmental factors, these systems reduce energy costs and minimize the environmental impact of pool operations.

Enhancing User Satisfaction with AI

AI technologies are enhancing user satisfaction by providing personalized experiences and ensuring optimal pool conditions.

1. Personalized Settings: AI-driven systems can learn user preferences and adjust pool settings accordingly. For example, these systems can customize water temperature, lighting, and filtration schedules based on user habits and preferences, providing a tailored and enjoyable experience.

2. User Feedback Analysis: AI algorithms can analyze user feedback and satisfaction data to identify areas for improvement. These insights help pool operators make informed decisions to enhance the overall user experience and address any issues promptly.

3. Predictive Maintenance: AI-powered predictive maintenance systems ensure that pool equipment and systems are maintained proactively, preventing issues before they occur. This proactive approach minimizes downtime and ensures that pools remain in optimal condition, enhancing user satisfaction.

Case Studies: AI in Pool Operations and Management

This section will showcase several case studies demonstrating the successful implementation of AI-driven pool operations and management solutions. These real-world examples highlight the benefits of AI technologies in optimizing pool performance, resource management, and user satisfaction.

Overcoming Challenges in AI-Enhanced Operations and Management

Implementing AI-driven pool operations and management systems comes with its own set of challenges. Addressing these challenges is crucial to fully realize the benefits of AI in pool operations:

1. System Integration: Integrating AI technologies with existing pool systems can be complex. Pool owners and operators should work with experienced professionals to ensure seamless integration and compatibility.

2. Data Management: Effective data management is essential for AI-driven systems. Pool owners and operators must ensure that their systems are capable of handling and processing large volumes of data, maintaining accuracy and reliability.

3. Cost: The cost of implementing advanced AI-driven operations and management systems can be high. Exploring financing options, government incentives, and partnerships with technology providers can help make these solutions more accessible.

4. User Training: Proper training is essential for pool owners and operators to fully utilize AI-driven operations and management systems. Comprehensive training programs and ongoing support can help users maximize the benefits of these advanced technologies.

Conclusion

AI-driven pool operations and management solutions are transforming the way swimming pools are managed and maintained. By optimizing performance, resource management, and user satisfaction, these technologies ensure efficient and effective pool operations. As we continue to explore and embrace AI advancements, the future of pool operations and management looks brighter and more innovative than ever before.

Chapter 12: AI in Pool Marketing and Customer Engagement

Marketing and customer engagement are essential for attracting and retaining pool users, as well as promoting pool-related services and products. AI technologies are revolutionizing pool marketing and customer engagement, offering advanced tools and capabilities for targeting, personalization, and interaction. This chapter explores how AI is transforming pool marketing and customer engagement, providing innovative solutions for pool businesses and operators.

AI-Driven Marketing Strategies

AI-powered marketing strategies enable pool businesses to target and engage customers more effectively, increasing visibility and driving growth.

1. Targeted Advertising: AI algorithms analyze customer data and behavior to create targeted advertising campaigns. These campaigns can reach specific audiences based on demographics, interests, and online activity, ensuring that marketing efforts are more effective and efficient.

2. Personalized Marketing: AI-driven personalization tools tailor marketing messages and offers to individual customers. By analyzing customer preferences and purchase history, these systems can deliver personalized content that resonates with each customer, increasing engagement and conversion rates.

3. Predictive Analytics: AI-powered predictive analytics tools forecast customer behavior and trends, enabling pool businesses to make data-driven marketing decisions. These insights help businesses identify new opportunities, optimize marketing strategies, and stay ahead of the competition.

Enhancing Customer Engagement with AI

AI technologies are enhancing customer engagement by providing personalized and interactive experiences, ensuring that customers feel valued and connected.

1. **Chatbots and Virtual Assistants:** AI-powered chatbots and virtual assistants provide instant customer support and information. These tools can answer queries, assist with bookings, and offer personalized recommendations, enhancing the overall customer experience.

2. **Social Media Engagement:** AI-driven social media tools analyze customer interactions and sentiment, helping businesses engage with their audience more effectively. These tools can identify trending topics, suggest content, and automate social media posts, ensuring consistent and meaningful engagement.

3. **Customer Feedback Analysis:** AI algorithms analyze customer feedback and reviews to identify areas for improvement. These insights help businesses understand customer needs and preferences, enabling them to make informed decisions and enhance the overall customer experience.

Case Studies: AI in Pool Marketing and Customer Engagement

This section will showcase several case studies demonstrating the successful implementation of AI-driven marketing and customer engagement solutions. These real-world examples highlight the benefits of AI technologies in attracting and retaining customers, increasing engagement, and driving business growth.

Overcoming Challenges in AI-Enhanced Marketing and Engagement

Implementing AI-driven marketing and customer engagement

systems comes with its own set of challenges. Addressing these challenges is crucial to fully realize the benefits of AI in pool marketing and customer engagement:

1. Data Privacy: AI-driven marketing and engagement tools require access to customer data, raising privacy concerns. Pool businesses must ensure that their systems comply with data privacy regulations and implement measures to protect customer data, such as data encryption and access controls.

2. Integration with Existing Systems: Integrating AI technologies with existing marketing and customer engagement systems can be complex. Businesses should work with experienced professionals to ensure seamless integration and compatibility.

3. Cost: The cost of implementing advanced AI-driven marketing and engagement systems can be high. Exploring financing options, government incentives, and partnerships with technology providers can help make these solutions more accessible.

4. User Training: Proper training is essential for businesses to effectively use AI-driven marketing and engagement systems. Comprehensive training programs and ongoing support can help users maximize the benefits of these advanced technologies.

Conclusion

AI-driven marketing and customer engagement solutions are transforming the way pool businesses attract and retain customers. By offering targeted advertising, personalized marketing, and enhanced customer engagement, these technologies ensure that businesses can effectively reach and connect with their audience. As we continue to explore and embrace AI advancements, the future of pool marketing and customer engagement looks brighter and more innovative than ever before.

Chapter 13: AI in Pool Supply Chain and Logistics

Efficient supply chain management and logistics are crucial for the pool industry to ensure timely delivery of materials, equipment, and chemicals. AI technologies are transforming supply chain and logistics processes, offering advanced tools for optimizing inventory management, transportation, and supplier relationships. This chapter explores how AI is enhancing supply chain and logistics in the pool industry, ensuring smooth and efficient operations.

AI-Enhanced Supply Chain Management

AI-driven supply chain management systems provide pool businesses with advanced tools for optimizing inventory, forecasting demand, and managing suppliers.

1. Inventory Optimization: AI algorithms analyze sales data, seasonal trends, and usage patterns to optimize inventory levels. These systems can predict demand for pool supplies and equipment, ensuring that businesses maintain optimal stock levels and reduce the risk of overstocking or stockouts.

2. Demand Forecasting: AI-powered demand forecasting tools use machine learning to predict future demand for pool products. By analyzing historical data and market trends, these tools help businesses make informed decisions about purchasing and production, ensuring they can meet customer demand.

3. Supplier Management: AI systems can evaluate and manage supplier performance, identifying the most reliable and cost-effective suppliers. These systems can also automate supplier communications and order processing, streamlining procurement and reducing lead times.

AI-Optimized Logistics

AI technologies are enhancing logistics processes, ensuring timely and efficient delivery of pool supplies and equipment.

1. Route Optimization: AI-driven route optimization tools analyze traffic patterns, weather conditions, and delivery schedules to determine the most efficient routes for transportation. These tools help reduce fuel consumption, delivery times, and transportation costs.

2. Real-Time Tracking: AI-powered tracking systems provide real-time visibility into the location and status of shipments. These systems enable businesses to monitor deliveries, predict arrival times, and quickly address any issues that arise, ensuring timely and reliable deliveries.

3. Automated Warehousing: AI-enhanced automated warehousing systems use robotics and machine learning to streamline warehouse operations. These systems can manage inventory, pick and pack orders, and coordinate shipping, improving efficiency and reducing labor costs.

Case Studies: AI in Pool Supply Chain and Logistics

This section will showcase several case studies demonstrating the successful implementation of AI-driven supply chain and logistics solutions. These real-world examples highlight the benefits of AI technologies in optimizing inventory management, transportation, and supplier relationships.

Overcoming Challenges in AI-Enhanced Supply Chain and Logistics

Implementing AI-driven supply chain and logistics systems comes with its own set of challenges. Addressing these challenges is crucial to fully realize the benefits of AI in the pool industry:

1. **Integration with Existing Systems:** Integrating AI technologies with existing supply chain and logistics systems can be complex. Businesses should work with experienced professionals to ensure seamless integration and compatibility.

2. **Data Accuracy:** The accuracy of AI-driven supply chain and logistics systems depends on the quality of the data they analyze. Ensuring accurate and up-to-date data is essential for these systems to function effectively.

3. **Cost:** The cost of implementing advanced AI-driven supply chain and logistics systems can be high. Exploring financing options, government incentives, and partnerships with technology providers can help make these solutions more accessible.

4. **User Training:** Proper training is essential for businesses to effectively use AI-driven supply chain and logistics systems. Comprehensive training programs and ongoing support can help users maximize the benefits of these advanced technologies.

Conclusion

AI-driven supply chain and logistics solutions are transforming the way pool businesses manage inventory, transportation, and supplier relationships. By optimizing inventory levels, forecasting demand, and streamlining logistics, these technologies ensure efficient and reliable operations. As we continue to explore and embrace AI advancements, the future of supply chain and logistics in the pool industry looks brighter and more innovative than ever before.

Chapter 14: AI in Pool Finance and Accounting

Managing finances and accounting effectively is essential for the success of any pool business. AI technologies are enhancing finance and accounting processes, providing advanced tools for financial planning, analysis, and management. This chapter explores how AI is transforming pool finance and accounting, offering innovative solutions for financial optimization and decision-making.

AI-Driven Financial Planning and Analysis

AI-powered financial planning and analysis tools provide pool businesses with advanced capabilities for budgeting, forecasting, and performance monitoring.

1. Budgeting and Forecasting: AI algorithms analyze historical financial data and market trends to create accurate budgets and forecasts. These tools can predict future revenue and expenses, helping businesses plan for growth and make informed financial decisions.

2. Performance Monitoring: AI-driven performance monitoring systems track key financial metrics and provide real-time insights into business performance. These systems can identify trends, anomalies, and opportunities for improvement, enabling businesses to optimize financial operations.

3. Financial Reporting: AI-powered financial reporting tools automate the creation of financial statements and reports. These tools ensure accuracy and compliance with accounting standards, reducing the time and effort required for financial reporting.

AI-Enhanced Accounting Processes

AI technologies are streamlining accounting processes, improving efficiency, accuracy, and compliance.

1. Automated Bookkeeping: AI-driven bookkeeping systems automatically categorize and record financial transactions. These systems can reconcile accounts, generate invoices, and manage accounts payable and receivable, reducing manual effort and minimizing errors.

2. Expense Management: AI-powered expense management tools analyze and track business expenses. These tools can identify patterns, detect anomalies, and provide recommendations for cost savings, ensuring that businesses manage expenses effectively.

3. Fraud Detection: AI algorithms can detect fraudulent activity by analyzing financial transactions and identifying unusual patterns. These systems help businesses prevent financial fraud and ensure the integrity of their financial data.

Case Studies: AI in Pool Finance and Accounting

This section will showcase several case studies demonstrating the successful implementation of AI-driven finance and accounting solutions. These real-world examples highlight the benefits of AI technologies in financial planning, analysis, and management.

Overcoming Challenges in AI-Enhanced Finance and Accounting

Implementing AI-driven finance and accounting systems comes with its own set of challenges. Addressing these challenges is crucial to fully realize the benefits of AI in pool finance and accounting:

1. Data Privacy: AI-driven finance and accounting tools require access to sensitive financial data, raising privacy concerns. Businesses must ensure that their systems comply with data privacy regulations and implement measures to protect financial data, such as data encryption and access controls.

2. Integration with Existing Systems: Integrating AI technologies with existing finance and accounting systems can be complex. Businesses should work with experienced professionals to ensure seamless integration and compatibility.

3. Cost: The cost of implementing advanced AI-driven finance and accounting systems can be high. Exploring financing options, government incentives, and partnerships with technology providers can help make these solutions more accessible.

4. User Training: Proper training is essential for businesses to effectively use AI-driven finance and accounting systems. Comprehensive training programs and ongoing support can help users maximize the benefits of these advanced technologies.

Conclusion

AI-driven finance and accounting solutions are transforming the way pool businesses manage their finances. By providing advanced tools for financial planning, analysis, and management, these technologies ensure efficient and effective financial operations. As we continue to explore and embrace AI advancements, the future of finance and accounting in the pool industry looks brighter and more innovative than ever before.

Chapter 15: The Future of AI in the Pool Industry

As AI technologies continue to evolve and advance, their impact on the pool industry will only grow. This chapter explores the future of AI in the pool industry, highlighting emerging trends, innovations, and opportunities for growth and improvement.

Emerging Trends in AI for Pools

Several emerging trends are set to shape the future of AI in the pool industry, offering new possibilities for enhancing pool design, construction, and management.

1. Advanced Predictive Analytics: AI-driven predictive analytics will become even more sophisticated, providing deeper insights into pool usage, maintenance needs, and customer preferences. These advancements will enable businesses to make more informed decisions and optimize their operations.

2. Integration with Smart Home Systems: AI technologies will increasingly integrate with smart home systems, creating seamless and interconnected pool environments. This integration will enhance user convenience, allowing for greater control and customization of pool settings and features.

3. Enhanced Sustainability: AI-driven solutions will play a crucial role in promoting sustainability in the pool industry. From optimizing energy and water usage to reducing chemical waste, AI technologies will help businesses minimize their environmental impact and operate more sustainably.

Innovations in AI for Pools

Innovations in AI will continue to drive advancements in pool design, construction, and management, offering new tools and capabilities for the industry.

1. Augmented Reality (AR) and Virtual Reality (VR): AI-powered AR and VR technologies will revolutionize the pool design process, allowing clients to visualize and interact with their pool designs in immersive and realistic ways. These technologies will enhance the design experience and enable more accurate and personalized pool creations.

2. Autonomous Pool Maintenance: The development of fully autonomous pool maintenance systems, powered by AI, will further streamline cleaning and maintenance processes. These systems will operate independently, ensuring pools remain clean and well-maintained with minimal human intervention.

3. AI-Powered Customer Experiences: AI technologies will enhance customer experiences by providing personalized recommendations, interactive interfaces, and seamless communication. From AI-driven pool design consultations to virtual pool tours, these innovations will improve customer engagement and satisfaction.

Opportunities for Growth and Improvement

The continued evolution of AI in the pool industry presents numerous opportunities for growth and improvement, benefiting businesses and customers alike.

1. Expanding Access to AI Technologies: As AI technologies become more affordable and accessible, a wider range of businesses will be able to leverage these advanced tools. This democratization of AI will drive innovation and competition, leading to better products and services for customers.

2. Enhancing Workforce Skills: The adoption of AI technologies will create new opportunities for workforce development, as businesses invest in training and education to equip their employees with the skills needed to effectively use AI tools. This will enhance job satisfaction and productivity, fostering a more skilled and knowledgeable workforce.

3. Driving Industry Standards: The widespread adoption of AI in the pool industry will drive the development of industry standards and best practices. These standards will ensure consistency, quality, and safety across the industry, benefiting businesses and customers alike.

Conclusion

The future of AI in the pool industry is bright and full of potential. As AI technologies continue to advance, they will transform every aspect of the industry, from design and construction to operations and customer engagement. By embracing these innovations, pool businesses can enhance their efficiency, sustainability, and customer satisfaction, paving the way for a more innovative and successful future.

The End

This concludes the comprehensive exploration of the role of AI in the pool industry, covering various aspects such as design, construction, operations, marketing, finance, and future trends. Embracing AI technologies promises a more innovative, efficient, and sustainable future for the pool industry.

www.ingramcontent.com/pod-product-compliance
Lightning Source LLC
Chambersburg PA
CBHW071957210526
45479CB00003B/971